Mission Praise Supplement

Compiled by
Peter Horrobin and Greg Leavers

WORDS EDITION

Marshall Pickering

First published in Great Britain in 1989 by Marshall Pickering
Reprinted 1990

Marshall Pickering is an imprint of the Collins Religious Division, part of the Collins Publishing Group, 8 Grafton Street, London W1X 3LA.

ISBN 0 551 018712 (Pack of 50)

Music edition ISBN 0 551 01872 0

Text set by Barnes Music Engraving Ltd., East Sussex, England
Printed by BPCC Hazell Books, Aylesbury, Bucks, England
Member of BPCC Ltd.

Foreword

This is the final collection of hymns and songs to be added to the Mission Praise stable before the production of a comprehensively indexed, combined edition embracing Volumes I, II and this Supplement.

Already Mission Praise is well established as a major book for praise and worship for thousands of churches in Great Britain and, indeed, across the world. This further selection ensures that there is an adequate range of both new and older material to be used throughout the church's year and at all personal or family occasions in the Christian life. Additionally there is a rich selection of newer praise and worship songs which have the hallmark of being of lasting significance.

We trust as with the earlier volumes this Supplement will further enhance the role of music in worship as a key means of bringing individuals into a dynamic and closer relationship with the living God.

Peter Horrobin and Greg Leavers
September 1989

648

Dave Bilbrough
© 1987 Thankyou Music

All hail the Lamb enthroned on high,
His praise shall be our battle cry.
He reigns victorious, for ever glorious,
His Name is Jesus, He is the Lord.

649

Tricia Richards
© 1987 Thankyou Music

1 **All heaven declares**
The glory of the risen Lord,
Who can compare,
With the beauty of the Lord?
For ever He will be,
The Lamb upon the throne.
I gladly bow the knee,
And worship Him alone.

2 I will proclaim,
The glory of the risen Lord.
Who once was slain,
To reconcile man to God.
For ever You will be,
The Lamb upon the throne,
I gladly bow the knee,
And worship You alone.

650

Chris Rolinson
© 1987 Thankyou Music

Almighty God, our heavenly Father,
We have sinned against You,
And against our fellow men.
In thought and word and deed,
Through negligence, through weakness,
Through our own deliberate fault.
We are truly sorry
And repent of all our sins.
For the sake of Your Son Jesus Christ,
Who died for us, who died for us,
    who died for us,
Forgive us all that is past;
And grant that we may serve You
In newness of life.
MEN   To the glory of Your Name,
WOMEN   To the glory of Your Name,
MEN   To the glory of Your Name,
WOMEN   To the glory of Your Name,
ALL   To the glory of Your Name.
        Amen, Amen.

651

Graham Kendrick
© 1988 Make Way Music / Thankyou Music

At this time of giving,
Gladly now we bring
Gifts of goodness and mercy
From a heavenly King.

1 Earth could not contain the treasures
Heaven holds for you,
Perfect joy and lasting pleasures,
Love so strong and true.
    At this time of giving . . .

2 May His tender love surround you
At this Christmastime;
May you see His smiling face
That in the darkness shines.
    At this time of giving . . .

3 But the many gifts He gives
Are all poured out from one;
Come receive the greatest gift,
The gift of God's own Son.
    At this time of giving . . .

Last two choruses and verses:
Lai, lai, lai . . . *(etc.)*

652

David J Evans
© 1986 Thankyou Music

1 **Be still,**
For the presence of the Lord,
    The Holy One, is here;
Come bow before Him now
With reverence and fear:
In Him no sin is found –
We stand on holy ground.
Be still,
For the presence of the Lord,
    The Holy One, is here.

2 Be still,
For the glory of the Lord
    Is shining all around;
He burns with holy fire,
With splendour He is crowned:
How awesome is the sight –
Our radiant King of light!
Be still,
For the glory of the Lord
    Is shining all around.

3 Be still,
For the power of the Lord
    Is moving in this place:
He comes to cleanse and heal,
To minister His grace –
No work too hard for Him.
In faith receive from Him.
Be still,
For the power of the Lord
    Is moving in this place.

653

from Psalm 95
© Timothy Dudley-Smith

1 **Come, let us praise the Lord,**
With joy our God acclaim,
His greatness tell abroad
And bless His saving Name.
Lift high your songs
Before His throne
To whom alone
All praise belongs.

2 Our God of matchless worth,
Our King beyond compare,
The deepest bounds of earth,
The hills, are in His care.
He all decrees,
Who by His hand
Prepared the land,
And formed the seas.

3 In worship bow the knee,
Our glorious God confess;
The great Creator, He,
The Lord, our Righteousness.
He reigns unseen:
His flock He feeds
And gently leads
In pastures green.

4 Come, hear His voice today,
Receive what love imparts;
His holy will obey
And harden not your hearts.
His ways are best;
And lead at last,
All troubles past,
To perfect rest.

654

from Psalm 95
Sarah Turner-Smith
© Ears and Eyes Music

Come, let us worship our Redeemer,
Let us bow down before His throne;
Come, let us kneel before our Maker
Holy is His Name.

1 Come into His presence with thanksgiving,
Make a joyful noise
For the Lord is a great God
King above all gods.
Come let us worship . . .

2 We are the people of His pasture,
The sheep of His hand,
For Christ the Lord is our Shepherd,
He will lead us home.
Come let us worship . . .

3 All praises be to God the Father,
Praise to Christ His Son;
Praise be to God the Holy Spirit:
Bless the Three-in-One!
Come let us worship . . .

655

© Timothy Dudley-Smith

1 **Come now with awe, earth's ancient**
 vigil keeping:
Cold under starlight lies the stony way.
Down from the hillside see the shepherds
 creeping,
Hear in our hearts the whispered news
 they say:
'Laid in a manger lies an infant sleeping,
Christ our Redeemer, born for us today.'

2 Come now with joy to worship and adore
 Him;
Hushed in the stillness, wonder and
 behold –
Christ in the stable where His mother bore
 Him,
Christ whom the prophets faithfully
 foretold:
High King of ages, low we kneel before
 Him,
Starlight for silver, lantern-light for gold.

3 Come now with faith, the age-long secret
 guessing,
Hearts rapt in wonder, soul and spirit
 stirred –
See in our likeness love beyond
 expressing,
All God has spoken, all the prophets
 heard;
Born for us sinners, bearer of all blessing,
Flesh of our flesh, behold the eternal
 Word!

4 Come now with love: beyond our
 comprehending
Love in its fullness lies in mortal span!
How should we love, whom Love is so
 befriending?
Love rich in mercy since our race began
Now stoops to save us, sighs and sorrows
 ending,
Jesus our Saviour, Son of God made man.

656

© 1987 Ruth Hooke

MEN **Come let us sing for joy to the Lord.**

WOMEN Come let us sing for joy to the Lord.

MEN We will sing, we will sing, we will sing.

WOMEN We will sing, we will sing, we will sing.

MEN Let us shout aloud
to the Rock of our salvation.

WOMEN Let us shout aloud
to the Rock of our salvation.

MEN We will shout! We will shout!
We will shout!

WOMEN We will shout! We will shout!
We will shout!

ALL For the Lord is the great God,
the great King above all gods.

MEN Splendour and majesty,

WOMEN Splendour and majesty,

MEN Are before Him,

WOMEN Are before Him.

MEN Strength and glory,

WOMEN Strength and glory,

ALL Are in His sanctuary.

657

After M MacDonald (1789–1872)
L Macbean (1853–1931)

1 **Child in the manger, infant of Mary,**
Outcast and stranger, Lord of all!
Child who inherits all our transgressions,
All our demerits on Him fall.

2 Once the most holy child of salvation
Gentle and lowly lived below:
Now as our glorious mighty Redeemer,
See Him victorious over each foe.

3 Prophets foretold Him, infant of wonder;
Angels behold Him on His throne:
Worthy our Saviour of all their praises;
Happy for ever are His own.

658

Graham Kendrick
© 1985 Make Way Music / Thankyou Music

1 **Darkness like a shroud**
Covers the earth,
Evil like a cloud
Covers the people;
But the Lord will rise upon you,
And His glory will appear on you,
Nations will come to your light.
Arise, shine, your light has come,
The glory of the Lord has risen on you;
Arise, shine, your light has come –
Jesus the light of the world has come.

2 Children of the light,
Be clean and pure;
Rise, you sleepers,
Christ will shine on you:
Take the Spirit's flashing two-edged sword
And with faith declare God's mighty word;
Stand up, and in His strength be strong!
Arise, shine . . .

3 Here among us now,
Christ the Light
Kindles brighter flames
In our trembling hearts:
Living Word, our lamp,
come guide our feet –
As we walk as one in light and peace,
Justice and truth shine like the sun.
Arise, shine . . .

4 Like a city bright,
So let us blaze;
Lights in every street
Turning night to day:
And the darkness shall not overcome,
Till the fullness of Christ's kingdom comes,
Dawning to God's eternal day.
Arise, shine, your light has come,
The glory of the Lord has risen on you;
Arise, shine, your light has come –
Jesus the light of the world,
Jesus the light of the world,
Jesus the light of the world has come.

659

Bob McGee
© 1976 Christian Arts Music / Word Music (UK)

Emmanuel, Emmanuel,
His name is called Emmanuel –
God with us,
Revealed in us –
His name is called Emmanuel.

660

from Luke 2
© Timothy Dudley-Smith

1 **Faithful vigil ended,**
Watching, waiting cease:
Master, grant Your servant
His discharge in peace.

2 All the Spirit promised,
All the Father willed,
Now these eyes behold it
Perfectly fulfilled.

3 This Your great deliverance
Sets Your people free;
Christ their light uplifted
All the nations see.

4 Christ, Your people's glory!
   Watching, doubting cease:
   Grant to us Your servants
   Our discharge in peace.

661
Bob Fitts
© 1985 Scripture in Song / Thankyou Music

Father in heaven, how we love You,
We lift Your Name in all the earth.
May Your kingdom be established in our
        praises
As Your people declare Your mighty
        works.
Blessèd be the Lord God Almighty,
Who was and is and is to come,
Blessèd be the Lord God Almighty,
Who reigns for evermore.

662
Dave Bilbrough
© 1985 Thankyou Music

1 **Father in heaven,**
   Our voices we raise:
   Receive our devotion,
   Receive now our praise
   As we sing of the glory
   Of all that You've done –
   The greatest love-story
   That's ever been sung.
       And we will crown You Lord of all,
       Yes, we will crown You Lord of all,
       For You have won the victory:
       Yes, we will crown You Lord of all.

2 Father in heaven,
   Our lives are Your own;
   We've been caught by a vision
   Of Jesus alone –
   Who came as a servant
   To free us from sin:
   Father in heaven,
   Our worship we bring.
       And we will crown . . .

3 We will sing Alleluia,
   We will sing to the King,
   To our mighty Deliverer
   Our alleluias will ring.
   Yes, our praise is resounding
   To the Lamb on the throne:
   He alone is exalted
   Through the love He has shown.
       And we will crown . . .

663
Graham Kendrick
© 1988 Make Way Music / Thankyou Music

1 **Father, never was love so near;**
   Tender, my deepest wounds to heal.
   Precious to me,
   Your gift of love;
   For me You gave
   Your only Son.
       And now thanks be to God
       For His gift beyond words,
       The Son whom He loved,
       No, He did not withhold Him,
       But with Him gave everything.
       Now He's everything to me.

2 Jesus, the heart of God revealed,
   With us, feeling the pain we feel.
   Cut to the heart,
   Wounded for me,
   Taking the blame,
   Making me clean.
       And now thanks be to God . . .

664
Graham Kendrick
© 1988 Make Way Music / Thankyou Music

WOMEN
1 **For God so loved the world**
   That He gave His only Son;
   And all who believe in Him
   Shall not die,
   But have eternal life;
   No, they shall not die,
   But have eternal life.

ALL
2 And God showed His love for you,
   When He gave His only Son;
   And you, if you trust in Him,
   Shall not die,
   But have eternal life;
   No you shall not die,
   But have eternal life.

665
David J Hadden
© Restoration Music Ltd

1 **For unto us a child is born,**
   Unto us a son is given,
   And the government
        shall be upon His shoulder;
   For unto us a child is born,
   Unto us a son is given,
   And the government
        shall be upon His shoulder.
       And He will be called Wonderful,
       Wonderful Counsellor, Mighty God,
       The Everlasting Father, Prince of peace,
       Mighty God.

2 And there shall be no end
To the increase of His rule,
To the increase of His government
   and peace;
For He shall sit on David's throne
Upholding righteousness,
Our God shall accomplish this.
   And He will be called Wonderful,
   Wonderful Counsellor, Mighty God,
   The Everlasting Father, Prince of peace,
   Mighty God.

3 For He is the Mighty God,
He is the Prince of peace,
The King of kings and Lord of lords:
All honour to the King,
All glory to His name,
For now and for evermore!
   And He will be called . . .

666
Graham Kendrick
© 1987 Make Way Music / Thankyou Music

1 **From the sun's rising**
Unto the sun's setting,
Jesus our Lord
Shall be great in the earth;
And all earth's kingdoms
Shall be His dominion –
All of creation
Shall sing of His worth.
   Let every heart, every voice,
   Every tongue join with spirits ablaze;
   One in His love,
   We will circle the world
   With the song of His praise.
   O let all His people rejoice,
   And let all the earth hear His voice!

2 To every tongue, tribe
And nation He sends us,
To make disciples,
To teach and baptize;
For all authority
To Him is given;
Now as His witnesses
We shall arise.
   Let every heart . . .

3 Come let us join with
The church from all nations,
Cross every border,
Throw wide every door;
Workers with Him
As He gathers His harvest,
Till earth's far corners
Our Saviour adore.
   Let every heart . . .

   Let all His people rejoice,
   And let all the earth hear His voice!

667
Mark Hayes
© 1983 Word Music (UK)

1 **Give thanks to the Lord for He is good,**
His love endures for ever.
Give thanks to the God of gods.
His love endures for ever.
O give thanks to the Lord of lords.
His love endures for ever.
To Him alone who does great works.
His love endures for ever.

2 By His understanding made the heavens,
His love endures for ever.
Who made the great and shining lights,
His love endures for ever.
The mighty sun to rule the day,
His love endures for ever.
And the moon and the stars to rule at night.
His love endures for ever.
   Hallelujah, Hallelu,
   The Lord Jehovah reigns.
   He is the same from age to age;
   His love will never change.

3 God led His children through the
   wilderness.
His love endures for ever.
And struck down many mighty kings,
His love endures for ever.
And gave to them an inheritance,
His love endures for ever.
A promised land for Israel.
His love endures for ever.
   Hallelujah . . .

4 He remembered us in our low estate
His love endures for ever.
And freed us from our enemies.
His love endures for ever.
To every creature He gives food.
His love endures for ever.
Give thanks to the God of heaven.
His love endures for ever.
His love endures for ever.
His love endures for ever.

668
Danny Daniels
© 1987 Mercy Music / Thankyou Music

1 **Glory, glory in the highest,**
Glory, to the Almighty;
Glory to the Lamb of God,
And glory to the living Word;
Glory to the Lamb!
MEN   I give glory
WOMEN Glory
MEN   Glory
WOMEN Glory
MEN   Glory
ALL   Glory to the Lamb!

669

Philip Coutts
© Oxford University Press

1 **God of all ages and Lord for all time,**
Creator of all things in perfect design:
For fields ripe for harvest, for rich golden
   grain,
For beauty in nature, we thank You again.

2 God of all nations and Lord of all lands,
Who placed the world's wealth in the palm
   of our hands,
We pray for Your guidance to guard
   against greed.
Though great the resources, still great is
   the need.

3 God of compassion and Lord of all life,
We pray for Your people in conflict and
   strife.
The earth You created a vast treasure
   store,
Yet hunger still thrives while men fight to
   gain more.

4 God of all wisdom, take us by the hand
And insight bestow when we ruin Your
   land.
For rivers polluted, for forests laid bare,
We pray Your forgiveness for failing to
   care.

5 God of all greatness and giver of light,
With each sunlit morning we worship Your
   might,
Our half-hearted service Your only
   reward:
For love beyond measure, we thank You O
   Lord.

670

Danny Reed
© 1987 Thankyou Music

Glorious Father we exalt You.
We worship, honour and adore You.
We delight to be in Your presence O Lord.
We magnify Your Holy Name,
And we sing come Lord Jesus,
Glorify Your Name,
And we sing come Lord Jesus,
Glorify Your Name.

671

Steve McEwan
© 1985 Dawn Treader Music /
Friends First Music / Word Music (UK)

**Great is the Lord and most worthy of
   praise,**
The city of our God, the holy place,
The joy of the whole earth.
Great is the Lord in whom we have the
   victory,
He aids us against the enemy,
We bow down on our knees.

And Lord, we want to lift Your name on
   high,
And Lord, we want to thank You,
For the works You've done in our lives;
And Lord, we trust in Your unfailing love,
For You alone are God eternal,
Throughout earth and heaven above.

672

Geoffrey Marshall-Taylor

Go, tell it on the mountain,
Over the hills and everywhere;
Go, tell it on the mountain
That Jesus is His Name.

1 He possessed no riches,
   no home to lay His head;
He saw the needs of others
   and cared for them instead.
Go tell it on the mountain . . .

2 He reached out and touched them,
   the blind, the deaf, the lame;
He spoke and listened gladly
   to anyone who came.
Go tell it on the mountain . . .

3 Some turned away in anger,
   with hatred in the eye;
They tried Him and condemned Him,
   then led Him out to die.
Go tell it on the mountain . . .

4 'Father, now forgive them' –
   those were the words He said;
In three more days He was alive
   and risen from the dead.
Go tell it on the mountain . . .

5 He still comes to people,
   His life moves through the lands;
He uses us for speaking,
   He touches with our hands.
Go tell it on the mountain . . .

673

Marilyn Baker
© 1982 Springtide / Word Music (UK)

1 **God came among us, He became a
   man,**
Became a baby, though through Him the
   world began.
He came to earth to bring us peace,
But where is that peace today?
It can be found
By those who will let Him direct their way.

2 He came to serve, to show us how much He
      cared;
  Our joys and sorrows He so willingly
      shared.
  He came to earth to bring us joy,
  But where is that joy today?
  It can be found
  By those who let Him wash their guilt away.

3 Death tried to hold Him, but it could not
      succeed;
  He rose again, and now we can be freed.
  He longs to give eternal life
  To all who will simply receive,
  Yes to all who
  Will open their hearts and just believe.

674
Steve and Gina Southworth
© 1985 Mercy Publishing / Thankyou Music
**'Hallelujah' sing to the Lord songs of
    praise;**
We bless You, Lord,
We give to You glory due Your holy Name.
We stretch out our hands,
    we stretch out our hands unto You,
    Lord;
We lift up our voice,
We lift up our voice
    inviting You into this place.
Hear us, O God;
As one, we bring our praise.
A pleasing sacrifice to You,
O Ancient of Days;
Ancient of Days.

675
Graham Kendrick
© 1987 Make Way Music / Thankyou Music
**He has shown you, O man,
    what is good –**
And what does the Lord require of you?
He has shown you, O man, what is good –
And what does the Lord require of you,
But to act justly, and to love mercy,
And to walk humbly with your God;
But to act justly, and to love mercy,
And to walk humbly with your God.
He has shown . . .

676
Jimmy Owens
© Lexicon Music Incorporated / M.P.I.
1 **He is born, our Lord and Saviour:**
  He is born, our heavenly King:
  Give Him honour, give Him glory,
  Earth rejoice and heaven sing!
  Born to be our sanctuary,
  Born to bring us light and peace;
  For our sins to bring forgiveness,
  From our guilt to bring release.

2 He who is from everlasting
  Now becomes the incarnate Word;
  He whose name endures for ever
  Now is born the Son of God:
  Born to bear our griefs and sorrows,
  Born to banish hate and strife;
  Born to bear the sin of many,
  Born to give eternal life!

3 Hail, the holy One of Israel,
  Chosen heir to David's throne;
  Hail the brightness of His rising –
  To His light the gentiles come:
  Plunderer of Satan's kingdom,
  Downfall of his evil power;
  Rescuer of all His people,
  Conqueror in death's dark hour!

4 He shall rule with righteous judgement,
  And His godly rule extend;
  Governor among the nations,
  His great kingdom has no end:
  He shall reign, the King of glory,
  Higher than the kings of earth –
  Alleluia, alleluia!
  Praise we now His holy birth!

677
Twila Paris
© 1976 Word Music (UK)
He is exalted,
The King is exalted on high.
I will praise Him.
He is exalted,
For ever exalted
And I will praise His Name!

He is the Lord.
For ever His truth shall reign.
Heaven and earth
Rejoice in His holy Name.
He is exalted,
The King is exalted on high.

678
Graham Kendrick
© Make Way Music / Thankyou Music
1 **He walked where I walk,**
  He stood where I stand,
  He felt what I feel,
  He understands.
  He knows my frailty,
  Shared my humanity,
  Tempted in every way,
  Yet without sin.
      God with us, so close to us,
      God with us, Immanuel!

2 One of a hated race,
  Stung by the prejudice,
  Suffering injustice,
  Yet He forgives.
  Wept for my wasted years,
  Paid for my wickedness,
  He died in my place,
  That I might live.
    God with us . . .

679
Chris A Bowater
© 1988 Lifestyle Music / Word Music (UK)
WOMEN
He who dwells, He who dwells
In the shelter of the most high,
MEN
He who dwells, He who dwells
In the shelter of the most high will
WOMEN
Rest in the shadow,
The shadow of the Almighty,
MEN
Will rest in the shadow,
The shadow of the Almighty.
ALL
And I'll say of the Lord He is my refuge.
And I'll say of the Lord He is my strength.
And I'll make of the most High one my
    dwelling-place.
And I'll say He is my God,
I'll say He is my God,
I will say He is my God in whom I trust.

680
Chris A Bowater
© 1986 Lifestyle Ministries / Word Music (UK)
1 **Holy Spirit, we welcome You,**
  Holy Spirit, we welcome You!
    Move among us with holy fire
    As we lay aside all earthly desire,
    Hands reach out and our hearts aspire.
  Holy Spirit, Holy Spirit,
  Holy Spirit, we welcome You!

2 Holy Spirit, we welcome You,
  Holy Spirit, we welcome You!
    Let the breeze of Your presence blow
    That Your children here might truly
        know
    How to move in the Spirit's flow.
  Holy Spirit, Holy Spirit,
  Holy Spirit, we welcome You!

3 Holy Spirit, we welcome You,
  Holy Spirit, we welcome You!
    Please accomplish in us today
    Some new work of loving grace,
      we pray –
    Unreservedly – have Your way.
  Holy Spirit, Holy Spirit,
  Holy Spirit, we welcome You!

681
Kelly Green
© 1988 Mercy Publishing / Thankyou Music
MEN AND WOMEN IN CANON
Holy is the Lord.
Holy is the Lord.
Holy is the Lord.
Holy is the Lord.
Righteousness and mercy,
Judgement and grace.
Faithfulness and sovereignty;
Holy is the Lord,
Holy is the Lord.

682
Carl Tuttle
© 1985 Mercy Publishing / Thankyou Music
1 **Hosanna, hosanna,**
    hosanna in the highest,
  Hosanna, hosanna, hosanna in the highest,
  Lord, we lift up Your name,
      with hearts full of praise.
  Be exalted, O Lord my God –
      Hosanna, in the highest.

2 Glory, glory, glory to the King of kings;
  Glory, glory, glory to the King of kings;
  Lord, we lift up Your name,
      with hearts full of praise.
  Be exalted, O Lord my God –
      glory to the King of kings.

683
© Timothy Dudley-Smith
1 **Holy child, how still You lie!**
  Safe the manger, soft the hay;
  Faint upon the eastern sky
  Breaks the dawn of Christmas Day.

2 Holy child, whose birthday brings
  Shepherds from their field and fold,
  Angel choirs and eastern kings,
  Myrrh and frankincense and gold:

3 Holy child, what gift of grace
  From the Father freely willed!
  In Your infant form we trace
  All God's promises fulfilled.

4 Holy child, whose human years
  Span like ours delight and pain;
  One in human joys and tears,
  One in all but sin and stain:

5 Holy child, so far from home,
  All the lost to seek and save:
  To what dreadful death You come,
  To what dark and silent grave!

6 Holy child, before whose Name
  Powers of darkness faint and fall;
  Conquered death and sin and shame –
  Jesus Christ is Lord of all!

7 Holy child, how still You lie!
  Safe the manger, soft the hay;
  Clear upon the eastern sky
  Breaks the dawn of Christmas Day.

684 Maggi Dawn
© 1987 Thankyou Music

1 **He was pierced for our transgressions,**
  And bruised for our iniquities;
  And to bring us peace He was punished,
  And by His stripes we are healed.

2 He was led like a lamb to the slaughter,
  Although He was innocent of crime;
  And cut off from the land of the living,
  He paid for the guilt that was mine.
    We like sheep have gone astray,
    Turned each one to his own way,
    And the Lord has laid on Him
    The iniquity of us all.
    We like sheep . . .

685 Psalm 84
Copyright controlled

How lovely is Thy dwelling-place,
  O Lord of hosts,
My soul longs and yearns for Your courts,
And my heart and flesh
  sing for joy to the living God.
One day in Thy presence
  is far better to me than gold,
Or to live my whole life somewhere else,
And I would rather be a door-keeper
  in Your house
Than to take my fate upon myself.
You are my sun and my shield,
You are my lover from the start,
And the highway to Your city
  runs through my heart.

686 © Brian Hoare / Jubilate Hymns

1 **I am the Bread,**
  The Bread of Life;
  Who comes to me will never hunger.
  I am the Bread,
  The Bread of heaven;
  Who feeds on me will never die.
    And as you eat, remember me –
    My body broken on the tree:
    My life was given to set you free,
    And I'm alive for evermore.

2 I am the Vine,
  The living Vine;
  Apart from me you can do nothing.
  I am the Vine,
  The real Vine:
  Abide in me and I in you.
    And as you drink, remember me –
    My blood was shed upon the tree:
    My life was given to set you free,
    And I'm alive for evermore.

3 So eat this bread,
  And drink this wine,
  And as you do, receive this life of mine.
  All that I am I give to you,
  That you may live for evermore.

687 Danny Daniels
© 1985 Mercy Publishing / Thankyou Music

I am a wounded soldier
  but I will not leave the fight,
Because the Great Physician is healing me.
So I'm standing in the battle,
  in the armour of His light,
Because His mighty power is real in me.
I am loved, I am accepted
  by the Saviour of my soul.
I am loved, I am accepted
  and my wounds will be made whole.

688 Marc Nelson
© 1988 Mercy Publishing / Thankyou Music

1 **I believe in Jesus**
  I believe He is the Son of God.
  I believe He died and rose again,
  I believe He paid for us all.
  And I believe He's here now
  Standing in our midst
  Here with the power to heal now
  And the grace to forgive.

2 I believe in You, Lord,
  I believe You are the Son of God;
  I believe You died and rose again:
  I believe You paid for us all:

MEN   And I believe You're here now,
WOMEN   I believe that You're here.
ALL   Standing in our midst.
MEN   Here with the power to heal now,
WOMEN   With the power to heal,
ALL   And the grace to forgive.

3   I believe in You, Lord . . . (All verse 2)
    And I believe He's here now . . .
              (2nd half of verse 1)

689

I look to the hills
From where shall my help come;
My help comes from the Lord,
Maker of Heaven and Earth.

1   He will not allow
    Your foot to ever slip
    He who keeps you will not sleep.
      I look to the hills . . .

2   He watches over you
    As your shade from moon and sun
    He will keep you from all harm.
      I look to the hills . . .

3   He will guard your ways
    As you come and as you go
    From this time and forever more.
      I look to the hills . . .

690

I rest in God alone,
From Him comes my salvation;
My soul finds rest in Him,
My fortress – I'll not be shaken.

1   My hope is in the Lord
    My honour and strength;
    My refuge is in Him for ever,
    My trust and all of my heart –
    In Him alone my soul finds rest.
      I rest in God alone . . .

2   O trust in Him, you people,
    Pour out your hearts,
    For God is our refuge for ever,
    My trust and all of my heart –
    In Him alone my soul finds rest.
    O trust in Him, you people . . .

691

1   I love You, O Lord, You alone,
    My refuge on whom I depend;
    My Maker, my Saviour, my own,
    My hope and my trust without end.
    The Lord is my strength and my song,
    Defender and Guide of my ways;
    My Master to whom I belong,
    My God who shall have all my praise.

2   The dangers of death gathered round,
    The waves of destruction came near;
    But in my despairing I found
    The Lord who released me from fear.
    I called for His help in my pain,
    To God my salvation I cried;
    He brought me His comfort again,
    I live by the strength He supplied.

3   The earth and the elements shake
    With thunder and lightning and hail;
    The cliffs and the mountaintops break
    And mortals are feeble and pale.
    His justice is full and complete,
    His mercy to us has no end
    The clouds are a path for His feet,
    He comes on the wings of the wind.

4   My hope is the promise He gives,
    My life is secure in His hand;
    I shall not be lost, for He lives!
    He comes to my side – I shall stand!
    Lord God, You are powerful to save,
    Your Spirit will spur me to pray;
    Your Son has defeated the grave:
    I trust and I praise You today!

692

1   I cannot count Your blessings, Lord,
      they're wonderful.
    I can't begin to measure Your great love.
    I cannot count the times You have forgiven
      me,
    And changed me by Your Spirit from
      above.
      How I worship You, my Father,
      You are wonderful.
      How I glorify You, Jesus,
      You're my Lord.
      How I praise You, Holy Spirit,
      You have changed my life,
      And You're now at work in me
      to change the world.

2 When I was blind You opened up my eyes
       to see.
   When I was dead You gave me life anew.
   When I was lost You found me and You
       rescued me,
   And carried me, rejoicing, home with You.
       How I worship You, my Father,
          You are wonderful.
       How I glorify You, Jesus,
          You're my Lord.
       How I praise You, Holy Spirit,
          You have changed my life,
       And You're now at work in me
          to change the world.

3 I cannot count Your mercies, Lord,
       they're marvellous.
   I can't begin to measure Your great grace.
   I cannot count the times that You have
       answered me,
   Whenever I have prayed and sought Your
       face.
       How I worship You . . .

4 Whenever I consider what I am to You,
   My heart is filled with wonder, love and
       awe.
   I want to share with others that You love
       them too,
   And tell the world of Jesus, more and
       more.
       How I worship You . . .

693
Chris Eaton
© 1983 Patch Music

1 **I see perfection**
       as I look in Your eyes, Lord;
   There's no rejection
       as I look in Your eyes, Lord.
   You are a river that is never dry,
   You are the star
       that lights the evening sky,
   You are my God and I will follow You,
   And now I know just where I'm going to.
       We are children, children of the King
       We will praise Your name,
       Glorify You, magnify You
       Jesus, we can never deny
       Your love for us on the cross
       Now You've made us
          children of the King.

2 Your Holy Spirit will for ever control me!
   I give my present, future, past,
       to You completely.
       You are a river . . .
       We are children . . .
       Now You've made us
          children of the King!

694
Colin Waller
© 1988 Oxford University Press

I want to thank You, I want to praise
   You,
   I want to love You more each day.
   I want to thank You, I want to praise You
   Yours is the power, the truth, the way.

1 Father, Your love I feel;
   Help me to show it to be real.
   Then I can openly say,
   Yours is the power, the truth, the way.
       I want to thank You . . .

2 Jesus, Your Word I hear;
   Help me to see its truth so clear.
   So I can openly say,
   Yours is the power, the truth, the way.
       I want to thank You . . .

3 Spirit, Your power I know;
   Help me to feel it, and to grow
   Stronger in every way, – 'cause
   Yours is the power, the truth, the way.
       I want to thank You . . . (twice)

695
Graham Kendrick
© 1988 Make Way Music / Thankyou Music

MEN   **'I will build my church,**
WOMEN I will build my church,
MEN   And the gates of hell,
WOMEN And the gates of hell,
MEN   Shall not prevail,
WOMEN Shall not prevail,
ALL   Against it.'
MEN   I will build . . .

ALL   *So you powers in the heavens*
               above,
          Bow down!
          And you powers on the earth
               below,
          Bow down!
          And acknowledge that Jesus,
          Jesus, Jesus is Lord,
          Is Lord!

696
Tommy Walker
© 1985 Thankyou Music

I will give You praise,
   I will sing Your song,
   I will bless Your holy Name;
   For there is no other God
   Who is like unto You,
   You're the only way,
   Only You are the Author of life,
   Only You, can bring the blind their sight,
   Only You, are called Prince of Peace,
   Only You promised You'd never leave.
   Only You are God.

697 Graham Kendrick
© 1987 Make Way Music / Thankyou Music

If my people who bear my name,
Will humble themselves and pray;
If they seek my presence
And turn their backs on their wicked ways;
Then I will hear from heaven,
I'll hear from heaven and will forgive.
I will forgive their sins
And will heal their land –
Yes I will heal their land.

698 Rob Hayward
© 1985 Thankyou Music

I'm accepted, I'm forgiven,
I am fathered by the true and living God.
I'm accepted, no condemnation,
I am loved by the true and living God.
There's no guilt or fear as I draw near
To the Saviour and Creator of the world.
There is joy and peace as I release
My worship to You, O Lord.

699 Graham Kendrick
© 1988 Make Way Music / Thankyou Music

Immanuel, O Immanuel,
Bowed in awe I worship at Your feet,
And sing Immanuel, God is with us,
Sharing my humanness, my shame,
Feeling my weaknesses, my pain,
Taking the punishment, the blame,
Immanuel.
And now my words cannot explain,
All that my heart cannot contain,
How great are the glories of Your Name.
Immanuel.

700 Chris Rolinson
© 1988 Thankyou Music

1 **I want to serve You, Lord,**
        in total abandonment,
   I want to yield my heart to You;
   I want to give my life in all surrender,
   I want to live for You alone.

2 I want to give my all
        in total abandonment,
   Releasing all within my grasp;
   I want to live my life in all its fulness,
   I want to worship Christ alone.

3 I want to come to You
        in total abandonment –
   Lord, will You set my heart ablaze?
   I want to love You with all my soul and
        strength,
   I want to give You all my days.

701 Michael Christ
© 1985 Mercy Music / Thankyou Music

It's Your blood that cleanses me,
It's Your blood that gives me life,
It's Your blood that took my place
In redeeming sacrifice,
And washes me whiter than the snow,
   than the snow.
My Jesus, God's precious sacrifice.

702 Scott Palazzo
© 1985 Mercy Publishing / Thankyou Music

I will magnify Thy Name
        above all the earth;
I will magnify Thy Name
        above all the earth.
I will sing unto Thee
        the praises in my heart;
I will sing unto Thee
        the praises in my heart.

703 © 1988 Ruth Hooke

I want to see Your face,
I want to see Your face,
Give You the worship of my heart, of my
        heart
Giving up my life to You.
Knowing You (knowing You),
Loving You (loving You), Lord.

704 Trish Morgan
© 1986 Thankyou Music

Jesus, I love You,
Love You more and more each day;
Jesus, I love You,
Your gentle touch renews my heart.
It's really no wonder why
No other love can satisfy,
Jesus, I love You,
You've won this heart of mine!

705 Chris A Bowater
© 1985 Lifestyle Music / Word Music (UK)

Jesus shall take the highest honour,
Jesus shall take the highest praise,
Let all earth join heaven in exalting
The Name which is above all other names.
Let's bow the knee in humble adoration
For at His name every knee must bow,
Let every tongue confess He is Christ,
        God's only Son.
Sovereign Lord we give you glory now,
For all honour and blessing and power
Belongs to You, belongs to You.

All honour and blessing and power
Belongs to You, belongs to You,
Lord Jesus Christ Son of the living God.

706 Peter and Diane Fung
© 1983 Thankyou Music

Jesus Christ our great Redeemer,
Mighty Victor and strong Deliverer,
King of kings and Lord of lords,
We praise You, praise Your name –
    Alleluia, alleluia;
King of kings and Lord of lords –
    Alleluia, alleluia!
Your victory is assured.

707 John Gibson
© 1987 Thankyou Music

Jesus, we celebrate Your victory,
Jesus, we revel in Your love,
Jesus, we rejoice You've set us free,
Jesus, Your death has brought us life.

1 It was for freedom that Christ has set us
    free,
No longer to be subject to a Yoke of
    slavery.
So we're rejoicing in God's victory,
Our hearts responding to His love.
    Jesus we celebrate . . .

2 His Spirit in us releases us from fear,
The way to Him is open, with boldness we
    draw near,
And in His presence our problems
    disappear,
Our hearts responding to His love.
    Jesus we celebrate . . .

708 I Watts (1674–1748)

1 **Joy to the world! The Lord has come:**
Let earth receive her King,
Let every heart prepare Him room
    And heaven and nature sing,
    And heaven and nature sing,
    And heaven,
        and heaven and nature sing!

2 Joy to the earth! The Saviour reigns:
Your sweetest songs employ
While fields and streams
    and hills and plains
Repeat the sounding joy,
Repeat the sounding joy,
Repeat, repeat the sounding joy.

3 He rules the world with truth and grace,
And makes the nations prove
The glories of His righteousness,
    The wonders of His love,
    The wonders of His love,
    The wonders, wonders of His love.

709 Dave Fellingham
© 1987 Thankyou Music

Jesus, You are the power,
You are the wisdom
That comes from the Lord God,
Who has revealed His love.

Our faith now rests on Your power Lord,
Which Your Spirit has poured out on us.
We declare the mystery hid before the
    ages,
Which God had planned for our glory.

For we have received a glorious
    inheritance
Pledged by the Spirit,
And our eyes have not seen,
And our ears have not heard,
What is in store for the hearts
Of the ones who love the Lord.

710 Merla Watson
© 1974 Gordon V. Thompson Music

Jehovah Jireh, my Provider,
His grace is sufficient for me,
    for me, for me.
Jehovah Jireh, my Provider,
His grace is sufficient for me.
My God shall supply all my needs
According to His riches in glory.
He will give His angels charge over me.
Jehovah Jireh cares for me, for me, for me.
Jehovah Jireh cares for me.

711 Graham Kendrick
© 1988 Make Way Music / Thankyou Music

Let it be to me according to Your Word.
Let it be to me according to Your Word.
I am Your servant, no rights shall I demand.
Let it be to me, let it be to me,
Let it be to me according to Your Word.

712
Graham Kendrick
© 1988 Make Way Music / Thankyou Music

1 **Like a candle flame,**
Flick'ring small in our darkness.
Uncreated light
Shines through infant eyes.
MEN   *God is with us, alleluia,*
WOMEN *God is with us, alleluia,*
MEN   *Come to save us, alleluia,*
WOMEN *Come to save us,*
ALL   *Alleluia!*

2 Stars and angels sing,
Yet the earth
Sleeps in the shadows;
Can this tiny spark
Set a world on fire?
    God is with us . . .

3 Yet His light shall shine
From our lives,
Spirit blazing,
As we touch the flame
Of His holy fire.
    God is with us . . .

713
Trish Morgan and others
© 1986 Thankyou Music

1 **Lord we long for You to move in power.**
There's a hunger deep within our hearts,
To see healing in our nation.
Send Your Spirit to revive us:
    Heal our nation!
    Heal our nation!
    Heal our nation!
    Pour out Your Spirit on this land!

2 Lord we hear Your Spirit coming closer,
A mighty wave to break upon our land,
Bringing justice, and forgiveness,
God we cry to You 'Revive us':
    Heal our nation . . .

714
Graham Kendrick
© 1987 Make Way Music / Thankyou Music

1 **Lord, the light of Your love is shining,**
In the midst of the darkness, shining:
Jesus, light of the world, shine upon us;
Set us free by the truth You now bring us –
Shine on me, shine on me.
    Shine, Jesus, shine,
    Fill this land with the Father's glory;
    Blaze, Spirit, blaze,
    Set our hearts on fire.
    Flow, river, flow,
    Flood the nations with grace and mercy;
    Send forth Your word, Lord,
    And let there be light!

2 Lord, I come to Your awesome presence,
From the shadows into Your radiance;
By Your Blood I may enter Your brightness:
Search me, try me, consume all my
    darkness –
Shine on me, shine on me.
    Shine, Jesus, shine . . .

3 As we gaze on Your kingly brightness
So our faces display Your likeness,
Ever changing from glory to glory:
Mirrored here, may our lives tell Your
    story –
Shine on me, shine on me.
    Shine, Jesus, shine . . .

715
Eddie Espinosa
© 1982 Mercy Publishing / Thankyou Music

Lord, I love You
You alone did hear my cry,
Only You can mend this broken heart of
    mine.
Yes, I love You,
And there is no doubt,
Lord, You've touched me from the inside
    out.

716
Chris Rolinson
© 1988 Thankyou Music

1 **Lord, come and heal Your church,**
Take our lives and cleanse with Your fire;
Let Your deliverance flow
As we lift Your name up higher.
    We will draw near
    And surrender our fear:
    Lift our hands to proclaim,
    'Holy Father, You are here!'

2 Spirit of God, come in
And release our hearts to praise You;
Make us whole, for
Holy we'll become and serve You,
    We will draw near . . .

3 Show us Your power, we pray,
That we may share in Your glory:
We shall arise, and go
To proclaim Your works most holy.
    We will draw near . . .

717
Graham Kendrick
© 1984 Make Way Music / Thankyou Music

1 **Look to the skies, there's a celebration;**
Lift up Your heads, join the angel song,
For our Creator becomes our Saviour,
As a baby born!
Angels amazed bow in adoration:
'Glory to God in the highest heaven!' –
Send the good news out to every nation,
For our hope has come.

> *Worship the King –*
> *come, see His brightness;*
> *Worship the King, His wonders tell:*
> *Jesus our King is born today –*
> *We welcome You, Emmanuel!*

2 Wonderful Counsellor, Mighty God,
Father for ever, the Prince of peace:
There'll be no end to Your rule of justice,
For it shall increase.
Light of Your face,
    come to pierce our darkness;
Joy of Your heart come to chase our gloom;
Star of the morning, a new day dawning,
Make our hearts Your home.
> *Worship the king . . .*

3 Quietly He came as a helpless baby –
One day in power He will come again;
Swift through the skies
    He will burst with splendour
On the earth to reign.
Jesus, I bow at Your manger lowly:
Now in my life let Your will be done;
Live in my flesh by Your Spirit holy
Till Your Kingdom comes.
> *Worship the king . . .*

718 Graham Kendrick
© 1985 Make Way Music / Thankyou Music

1 **Let all the earth hear His voice,**
Let the people rejoice
At the sound of His name;
Let all the valleys and hills burst with joy,
And the trees of the field
Clap their hands.
> *Justice and love*
> *He will bring to the world,*
> *His kingdom will never fail;*
> *Held like a two-edged sword*
> *in our hand,*
> *His word and truth shall prevail,*
> *shall prevail!*

2 Let all the earth hear His voice,
Let the prisoners rejoice –
He is coming to save.
Satan's dark strongholds crash down
As with prayer we surround,
As the cross we proclaim.
> *Justice and love . . .*

3 Let all the earth hear His song;
Sing it loud, sing it strong –
It's the song of His praise.
Silent no more, we cry out –
Let the world hear the shout:
In the earth the Lord reigns.
> *Justice and love . . .*

719 Graham Kendrick
© 1988 Make Way Music / Thankyou Music

1 **Light has dawned that ever shall blaze,**
Darkness flees away;
Christ the light has shone in our hearts,
Turning night to day.
> *We proclaim Him King of kings,*
> *We lift high His name;*
> *Heaven and earth shall bow at His feet,*
> *When He comes to reign.*

2 WOMEN
Saviour of the world is He,
Heaven's king come down;
Judgement, love and mercy meet
At His thorny crown.
ALL *We proclaim . . .*

3 MEN
Life has sprung from hearts of stone,
By the Spirit's breath;
Hell shall let her captives go,
Life has conquered death.
ALL *We proclaim . . .*

4 Blood has flowed that cleanses from sin,
God His love has proved;
Man may mock and demons may rage –
We shall not be moved!
> *We proclaim . . .*

> *We proclaim . . .*

720 Graham Kendrick
© 1988 Make Way Music / Thankyou Music

May our worship be acceptable
In Your sight, O Lord;
May our worship be acceptable
In Your sight, O Lord;
May the words of my mouth be pure,
And the meditation of my heart;
May our worship be acceptable
In Your sight, O Lord.

721 Mavis Ford
© Springtide / Word Music (UK)

Mighty in victory, glorious in majesty:
Every eye shall see Him when He appears,
Coming in the clouds
    with power and glory.
Hail to the King!
We must be ready, watching and praying,
Serving each other, building His kingdom;
Then every knee shall bow,
    then every tongue confess,
Jesus is Lord!

722
Graham Kendrick
© 1988 Make Way Music / Thankyou Music

1 **Now dawns the Sun of righteousness,**
And the darkness will never
His brightness dim;
True light that lights the hearts of men,
Only Son of the Father,
Jesus Christ.
Tell out, tell out the news,
On every street proclaim,
A child is born, a Son is given
And Jesus is His Name!
Tell out, tell out the news,
Our Saviour Christ has come,
In every tribe and nation,
Let songs of praise be sung,
Let songs of praise be sung!

2 Laughter and joy He will increase,
All our burdens be lifted,
Oppression cease;
The blood-stained battle-dress be burned,
And the art of our warfare
Never more be learned.
Tell out . . .

3 So let us go, His witnesses,
Spreading news of His kingdom
Of righteousness,
'Till the whole world has heard the song,
'Till the harvest is gathered,
Then the end shall come.
Tell out . . .

723
Graham Kendrick
© 1988 Make Way Music / Thankyou Music

1 LEADER **O come and join the dance**
That all began so long ago,
ALL When Christ the Lord was born in
Bethlehem.
LEADER Through all the years of darkness
Still the dance goes on and on,
ALL Oh, take my hand and come and
join the song.
MEN *Rejoice!*
WOMEN *Rejoice!*
MEN *Rejoice!*
WOMEN *Rejoice!*
ALL *O lift your voice and sing,*
And open up your heart to
welcome Him.
MEN *Rejoice!*
WOMEN *Rejoice!*
MEN *Rejoice!*
WOMEN *Rejoice!*
ALL *And welcome now your King,*
For Christ the Lord was born in
Bethlehem.

2 LEADER Come shed your heavy load
And dance your worries all away,
ALL For Christ the Lord was born in
Bethlehem.
LEADER He came to break the power of sin
And turn your night to day,
ALL Oh, take my hand and come and
join the song.
Rejoice . . .

3 *(Instrumental verse and chorus)*

4 LEADER Let laughter ring and angels sing
And joy be all around,
ALL For Christ the Lord was born in
Bethlehem.
LEADER And if you seek with all your heart
He surely can be found,
ALL Oh, take my hand and come and
join the song.
Rejoice . . .
Rejoice . . .
For Christ the Lord was born in
Bethlehem.
For Christ the Lord was born in
Bethlehem.

724
Dave Bilborough
© 1988 Thankyou Music

Oh, the joy of Your forgiveness,
Slowly sweeping over me;
Now in heartfelt adoration
This praise I'll bring to You my King,
I'll worship You my Lord.

725
Graham Kendrick
© 1988 Make Way Music / Thankyou Music

1 **O what a mystery I see,**
What marvellous design,
That God should come as one of us,
A Son in David's line.
Flesh of our flesh, of woman born,
Our humanness He owns;
And for a world of wickedness
His guiltless blood atones.

2 This perfect Man, incarnate God,
By selfless sacrifice
Destroyed our sinful history,
All fallen Adam's curse.
In Him the curse to blessing turns,
My barren spirit flowers,
As over the shattered power of sin
The cross of Jesus towers.

WOMEN
3 By faith a child of His I stand,
An heir in David's line,
Royal descendant by His blood
Destined by Love's design.
MEN
Fathers of faith, my fathers now!
Because in Christ I am,
ALL
And all God's promises in Him
To me are 'Yes, Amen'!

4 No more then as a child of earth
Must I my lifetime spend –
His history, His destiny
Are mine to apprehend.
Oh what a Saviour, what a Lord,
O Master, Brother, Friend!
What miracle has joined me to
This life that never ends!

726 © 1989 Greg Leavers

1 **Oh Lord, I turn my mind to You**
Right away from the things that today I've
been through.
I'm so sorry Lord when they've clouded
the way
And then have stopped me trusting You.

2 Oh Lord, I turn my eyes to You
And see love in Your eyes as You look
towards me.
I'm so unworthy Lord, yet You died for me;
All I can say is I love You.

3 Oh Lord, please speak Your Word to me,
Just the message I need, out of Your loving
heart.
May I grasp Your truth that will set my
heart free
From the things that hold me back.

4 Oh Lord, please fill my heart anew;
I surrender my pride which stops me
trusting You.
For I long that my life may glorify You;
I open up my life to You.

727
Michael Smith
© Meadowgreen Music Company /
EMI Publishing

O Lord, our Lord,
How majestic is Your name in all the earth;
O Lord, our Lord,
How majestic is Your name in all the earth;
O Lord, we praise Your name;
O Lord, we magnify Your name.

Prince of peace, mighty God,
O Lord God almighty!

728
Graham Kendrick
© 1987 Make Way Music / Thankyou Music

1 **O Lord, the clouds are gathering,**
The fire of judgement burns.
How we have fallen!
O Lord, You stand appalled to see
Your laws of love so scorned.
And lives so broken.
MEN   *Have mercy, Lord,*
WOMEN   *Have mercy, Lord.*
MEN   *Forgive us, Lord,*
WOMEN   *Forgive us, Lord.*
ALL   *Restore us, Lord;*
            Revive Your church again.
MEN   *Let justice flow,*
WOMEN   *Let justice flow,*
MEN   *Like rivers,*
WOMEN   *Like rivers;*
ALL   *And righteousness*
            Like a never-failing stream.

2 O Lord, over the nations now,
Where is the dove of peace?
Her wings are broken,
O Lord, while precious children starve,
The tools of war increase,
Their bread is stolen.
MEN   *Have mercy, Lord . . .*

3 O Lord, dark powers are poised
To flood our streets with hate and fear.
We must awaken!
O Lord, let love reclaim the lives
That sin would sweep away,
And let Your kingdom come!
MEN   *Have mercy, Lord . . .*

4 Yet, O Lord, Your glorious cross
Shall tower triumphant in this land,
Evil confounding;
Through the fire, Your suffering church
Display the glories of her Christ,
Praises resounding.
MEN   *Have mercy, Lord . . .*

            A never-failing stream.

729
Carl Tuttle
© 1982 Mercy Publishing / Thankyou Music

Open your eyes,
See the glory of the King;
Lift up your voice,
And His praises sing!

I love You, Lord,
I will proclaim:
Alleluia!
I bless Your name.

730
Graham Kendrick
© 1988 Make Way Music / Thankyou Music
Peace to you.
We bless you now in the name of the Lord.
Peace to you.
We bless you now
    in the name of the Prince of Peace.
Peace to you. Peace to you.
Peace to you. Peace to you.

Swing wide the gates,
Swing wide the gates.
Let the King come in,
Swing wide the gates,
Swing wide the gates,
Let the King come in.

731
Chris Bowater
© 1986 Word Music (UK)
Rejoice, rejoice, rejoice,
Rejoice, rejoice, rejoice;
My soul rejoices in the Lord.
Rejoice . . .

My soul magnifies the Lord,
And my spirit rejoices in God my Saviour;
My soul magnifies the Lord,
And my spirit rejoices in my God.
   Rejoice . . .

734
Graham Kendrick
© 1988 Make Way Music / Thankyou Music
1 **Show Your power, O Lord,**
Demonstrate the justice of Your kingdom;
Prove Your mighty word,
Vindicate Your name
Before a watching world.
Awesome are Your deeds, O Lord –
Renew them for this hour.
   Show Your power, O Lord –
   Among the people now.

2 Show Your power, O Lord,
Cause Your church to rise and take action;
Let all fear be gone,
Powers of the age to come
Are breaking through.
We Your people are ready to serve,
To arise and to obey.
   Show Your power, O Lord,
   And set the people –
   Show Your power, O Lord,
   And set the people –
   Show Your power, O Lord,
   And set the people free!

732
Dave Bilborough
© 1984 Thankyou Music
Reigning in all splendour –
Victorious love;
Christ Jesus the Saviour,
Transcendent above.
All earthly dominions
And kingdoms shall fall,
For His name is Jesus
And He is the Lord.
He is Lord, He is Lord,
He is Lord, He is Lord.

733
Chris Bowater
© 1986 Word Music
Swing wide the gates,
Let the King come in.
Swing wide the gates,
Make a way for Him.
Swing wide the gates,
Let the King come in.
Swing wide the gates,
Make a way for Him.

Here He comes,
The King of glory;
Here He comes,
Mighty in victory;
Here He comes
In splendour and majesty.

735
Graham Kendrick
© 1988 Make Way Music / Thankyou Music
1 **Such love, pure as the whitest snow;**
Such love weeps for the shame I know;
Such love, paying the debt I owe;
O Jesus, such love.

2 Such love, stilling my restlessness;
Such love, filling my emptiness;
Such love, showing me holiness;
O Jesus, such love.

3 Such love springs from eternity;
Such love, streaming through history;
Such love, fountain of life to me;
O Jesus, such love.

736
Chris Bowater
© 1978 Springtide / Word Music (UK)

Spirit of God, show me Jesus;
Remove the darkness,
   let truth shine through.
Spirit of God, show me Jesus;
Reveal the fullness of His love to me!

737
Paul Armstrong
© 1984 Restoration Music Ltd

Spirit of the living God fall afresh on me,
Spirit of the living God fall afresh on me,
Fill me anew, fill me anew,
Spirit of the Lord fall afresh on me.

738
Graham Kendrick
© 1988 Make Way Music / Thankyou Music

Soften my heart Lord, soften my heart;
From all indifference set me apart
To feel Your compassion,
To weep with Your tears –
Come soften my heart, O Lord,
   soften my heart.

739
Graham Kendrick
© 1985 Make Way Music / Thankyou Music

1 **Thank You for the cross,**
The price You paid for us,
How You gave Yourself
So completely,
Precious Lord. (Precious Lord.)
Now our sins are gone,
All forgiven,
Covered by Your blood,
All forgotten,
Thank You Lord (Thank You Lord)
Oh I love You Lord,
Really love You Lord.
I will never understand
Why You love me.
You're my deepest joy,
You're my heart's delight,
And the greatest thing of all,
O Lord, I see:
You delight in me!

2 For our healing there
Lord You suffered,
And to take our fear
You poured out Your love,
Precious Lord. (Precious Lord.)
Calvary's work is done,
You have conquered,
Able now to save
So completely,
Thank You Lord. (Thank You Lord.)
Oh I love You . . .

740
© David Mowbray / Jubilate Hymns

1 **Take heart and praise our God;**
Rejoice and clap your hands –
His power our foe subdued,
His mercy ever stands:
Let trumpets sound and people sing,
The Lord through all the earth is King!

2 Take heart, but sing with fear,
Exalt His worthy name;
With mind alert and clear
Now celebrate His fame:
Let trumpets sound . . .

3 Take heart for future days,
For tasks as yet unknown –
The God whose name we praise
Is seated on the throne:
Let trumpets sound . . .

4 Take heart and trust in God
The Father and the Son –
God is our strength and shield,
His Spirit guides us on:
Let trumpets sound . . .

741
Chris Bowater
© 1982 Word Music (UK)

The Lord has led forth His people with
joy,
And His chosen ones with singing, singing;
The Lord has led forth His people with joy,
And His chosen ones with singing.
He has given to them the lands of the
   nations,
To possess the fruit and keep His laws,
And praise, praise His name.
The Lord has led forth His people with joy,
And His chosen ones with singing, singing;
The Lord has led forth His people with joy,
And His chosen ones with singing.

742
Graham Kendrick
© 1983 Make Way Music / Thankyou Music

1 **The Lord is King,**
   He is mighty in battle,
Working wonders,
   Glorious in majesty.

2 The Lord is King –
   So majestic in power!
His right hand
   Has shattered the enemy.

3 A This is my God
   And I will praise Him;
B This is my God
   And I will praise Him:

4 ^A My strength and song
   And my salvation,
  ^B My strength and song
   And my salvation.

(*The singers may divide at* A *and* B)

743
Graham Kendrick
© 1988 Make Way Music / Thankyou Music

1 **This Child, secretly comes in the night,**
  Oh, this Child, hiding a heavenly light,
  Oh, this Child, coming to us like a stranger,
  This heavenly Child.
    This Child, heaven come down
      now to be with us here,
    Heavenly love and mercy appear,
    Softly in awe and wonder come near
    To this heavenly Child.

2 This Child, rising on us like the sun,
  Oh this Child, given to light everyone,
  Oh this Child, guiding our feet on the
      pathway
  To peace on earth.
    This Child, heaven come down . . .

3 This Child, raising the humble and poor,
  Oh this Child, making the proud ones to
      fall;
  This Child, filling the hungry with good
      things,
  This heavenly Child.
    This Child, heaven come down . . .

744
William Cowper 1731–1800

1 **There is a fountain filled with blood**
  Drawn from Emmanuel's veins;
  And sinners, plunged beneath that flood,
  Lose all their guilty stains.

2 The dying thief rejoiced to see
    That fountain in his day;
  And there may I, as vile as he,
    Wash all my sins away.

3 Dear dying Lamb! Your precious blood
    Shall never lose its power,
  Till all the ransomed Church of God
    Be saved, to sin no more.

4 E'er since, by faith, I saw the stream
    Your flowing wounds supply,
  Redeeming love has been my theme,
    And shall be till I die.

5 Then in a nobler, sweeter song,
    I'll sing Your power to save,
  When this poor lisping, stammering tongue
    Lies silent in the grave.

745
Graham Kendrick
© 1988 Make Way Music / Thankyou Music

1 **Tonight, while all the world was**
        sleeping,
  A light exploded in the skies.
  And then, as glory did surround us,
  A voice, an angel did appear!
  WOMEN *Glory to God in the highest,*
  MEN   *Glory to God in the highest,*
         And on the earth,
  ALL   *Be peace from heaven!*
  WOMEN *Glory to God in the highest,*
  MEN   *Glory to God in the highest,*
         And on the earth,
  ALL   *Be peace from heaven!*

2 Afraid, we covered up our faces,
  Amazed at what our ears did hear.
  Good news of joy for all the people –
  Today a Saviour has appeared!
    Glory to God . . .

  (Bridge)
  And so to Bethlehem
  To find it was all true;
  Despised and worthless shepherds,
  We were the first to know!
    Glory to God . . .

746
Chris A Bowater
© 1985 Lifestyle Ministries / Word Music

1 **The Spirit of the Lord,**
  The sovereign Lord, is on me
  Because He has anointed me
  To preach good news to the poor:
    Proclaiming Jesus, only Jesus –
    It is Jesus, Saviour, Healer and Baptizer,
    And the Mighty King,
      the Victor and Deliverer –
    He is Lord, He is Lord, He is Lord.

2 And He has called on me
  To bind up all the broken hearts,
  To minister release to every
  Captivated soul:
    Proclaiming Jesus . . .

3 Let righteousness arise
  And blossom as a garden;
  Let praise begin to spring in every
  Tongue and nation:
    Proclaiming Jesus . . .

747 John Daniels and Phil Thompson
© Eyes and Ears Music

1 **The earth was dark until You spoke –**
Then all was light and all was peace;
Yet still, O God, so many wait
To see the flame of love released.
  Lights to the world! O Light divine,
  Kindle in us a mighty flame,
  Till every heart, consumed by love
  Shall rise to praise Your holy Name!

2 In Christ You gave Your gift of life
To save us from the depth of the night:
O come and set our spirits free
And draw us to Your perfect light.
  Lights to the world . . .

3 Where there is fear may we bring joy
And healing to a world in pain:
Lord, build Your kingdom through our
    lives
Till Jesus walks this earth again.
  Lights to the world . . .

4 O burn in us, that we may burn
With love that triumphs in despair;
And touch our lives with such a fire
That souls may search and find You there.
  Lights to the world . . .

748 Graham Kendrick
© 1986 Make Way Music / Thankyou Music

MEN **The earth is the Lord's**
WOMEN And everything in it.
MEN The earth is the Lord's
WOMEN The work of His hands.
MEN The earth is the Lord's
WOMEN And everything in it.
ALL And all things were made for His
      glory!

1 The mountains are His,
The seas and the islands,
The cities and towns,
The houses and streets:
Let rebels bow down
And worship before Him,
For all things were made for His glory!
  MEN The earth is the Lord's . . .

2 The mountains are His,
  MEN The earth is the Lord's . . .

  MEN The earth is the Lord's
  WOMEN And everything in it.
  MEN The earth is the Lord's
  WOMEN The work of His hands.

MEN The earth is the Lord's
WOMEN And everything in it.
ALL And all things were made,
      Yes, all things were made,
      And all things were made for His
        glory!

749 Copyright control

1 **What a mighty God we serve . . .**

2 He created you and me . . .

3 He has all the power to save . . .

4 Let us praise the living God . . .

5 What a mighty God we serve . . .

750 Chris Rolinson
© 1988 Thankyou Music

1 MEN **We break this bread**
          to share in the body of Christ:
  WOMEN We break this bread
          to share in the body of Christ:
  ALL Though we are many,
      We are one body,
      Because we all share
      We all share in one bread.

2 MEN We drink this cup
          to share in the body of Christ:
  WOMEN We drink this cup
          to share in the body of Christ:
  ALL Though we are many,
      We are one body,
      Because we all share
      We all share in one cup.

751 Graham Kendrick
© 1988 Make Way Music / Thankyou Music

We shall stand,
  with our feet on the Rock;
Whatever men may say,
  we'll lift Your name up high –
And we shall walk
  through the darkest night;
Setting our faces like flint,
We'll walk into the light!

1 Lord, You have chosen me for fruitfulness
To be transformed into Your likeness:
I'm going to fight on through till I see You
Face to face.
  We shall stand . . .

2 Lord, as Your witnesses
   You've appointed us,
   And with Your Holy Spirit anointed us:
   And so I'll fight on through till I see You
   Face to face.
   We shall stand . . .

752 Adrian Snell
© 1986 Word Music (UK)

1 **We Your people bow before You**
   Broken and ashamed;
   We have turned on Your creation
   Crushed the life You freely gave.

2 Lord, have mercy on Your children
   Weeping and in fear:
   For You are our God and Saviour
   Father in Your love draw near.

3 Father, in this hour of danger
   We will turn to You:
   O forgive us, Lord, forgive us
   And our lives and faith renew.

4 Pour Your Holy Spirit on us,
   Set our hearts aflame:
   All shall see Your power in the nations
   May we bring glory to Your name.

753 Bryn and Sally Haworth
© 1983 Signalgrade Ltd

1 **What kind of love is this,**
   That gave itself for me?
   I am the guilty one,
   Yet I go free.
   What kind of love is this?
   A love I've never known.
   I didn't even know His Name,
   What kind of love is this?

2 What kind of man is this,
   That died in agony?
   He who had done no wrong
   Was crucified for me.
   What kind of man is this,
   Who laid aside His throne
   That I may know the love of God?
   What kind of man is this?

3 By grace I have been saved,
   It is the gift of God.
   He destined me to be His son,
   Such is His love.
   No eye has ever seen,
   No ear has ever heard,
   Nor has the heart of man conceived,
   What kind of love is this?

754 Graham Kendrick
© 1988 Make Way Music / Thankyou Music

1 **Who can sound the depths of sorrow**
   In the Father heart of God,
   For the children we've rejected,
   For the lives so deeply scarred?
   And each light that we've extinguished
   Has bought darkness to our land:
   Upon the nation, upon the nation
   Have mercy Lord!

2 We have scorned the truth You gave us,
   We have bowed to other lords,
   We have sacrificed the children
   On the altars of our gods.
   O let truth again shine on us,
   Let Your holy fear descend:
   Upon the nation, upon the nation
   Have mercy Lord!

MEN
3 Who can stand before Your anger;
   Who can face Your piercing eyes?
   For You love the weak and helpless,
   And You hear the victims' cries.
ALL
   Yes, You are a God of justice,
   And Your judgement surely comes:
   Upon the nation, upon the nation
   Have mercy Lord!

WOMEN
4 Who will stand against the violence?
   Who will comfort those who mourn?
   In an age of cruel rejection,
   Who will build for love a home?
ALL
   Come and shake us into action,
   Come and melt our hearts of stone:
   Upon Your people, upon Your people,
   Have mercy Lord!

5 Who can sound the depths of mercy
   In the Father heart of God?
   For there is a Man of sorrows
   Who for sinners shed His blood.
   He can heal the wounds of nations,
   He can wash the guilty clean:
   Because of Jesus, because of Jesus,
   Have mercy Lord!

755 Paul Field
© 1987 Thankyou Music

1 **With all my heart I thank You Lord.**
   With all my heart I thank You Lord,
   For this bread and wine we break,
   For this sacrament we take,
   For the forgiveness that You make,
   I thank You Lord.

2 With all my soul I thank You Lord.
With all my soul I thank You Lord,
For this victory that You've won,
For this taste of things to come,
For this love that makes us one,
I thank You Lord.

3 With all my voice I thank You Lord.
With all my voice I thank You Lord,
For the sacrifice of pain,
For the Spirit and the flame,
For the power of Your Name,
I thank You Lord.

756 Bill Yarger
© Maranatha! Music (USA) / Word Music (UK)
1 **Wonderful Counsellor Jesus:**
Search me, know me, Jesus;
Lead me, guide me, Jesus –
Wonderful Counsellor Jesus.

2 Mighty God, Son of God, Jesus;
Name above all other names, Jesus:
Glorify, magnify, Jesus –
Mighty God, Son of God, Jesus.

3 Everlasting Father, Jesus;
Holy and unchangeable, Jesus:
Fill me with Your presence, Jesus –
Everlasting Father, Jesus.

4 Prince of peace, rule my heart, Jesus;
Know my every anxious thought, Jesus;
Calm my fears, dry my tears, Jesus –
Prince of peace, rule my heart, Jesus.

5 Wonderful Counsellor Jesus;
Mighty God, Son of God, Jesus;
Everlasting Father, Jesus –
Prince of peace, rule my heart, Jesus.

757 Horatio G Spafford
1 **When peace like a river attendeth my
way,**
When sorrows like sea-billows roll;
Whatever my lot You have taught me to
say,
'It is well, it is well with my soul.'

2 Though Satan should buffet, if trials should
come,
Let this blessed assurance control,
That Christ has regarded my helpless
estate,
And has shed His own blood for my soul.

3 My sin – O the bliss of this glorious
thought –
My sin – not in part – but the whole
Is nailed to His Cross; and I bear it no
more;
Praise the Lord, praise the Lord, O my
soul.

4 For me, be it Christ, be it Christ hence to
live!
If Jordan above me shall roll.
No pang shall be mine, for in death as in
life
You will whisper Your peace to my soul.

5 But Lord, it's for You for Your coming we
wait,
The sky, not the grave, is our goal:
O, trump of the angel! O voice of the Lord!
Blessed hope! blessed rest of my soul.

758 Mark Altrogge
© 1986 People of Destiny
You are beautiful beyond description,
Too marvellous for words,
Too wonderful for comprehension,
Like nothing ever seen or heard.
Who can grasp Your infinite wisdom?
Who can fathom the depth of Your love?
You are beautiful beyond description,
Majesty, enthron'd above.
And I stand, I stand in awe of You.
I stand, I stand in awe of You.
Holy God, to whom all praise is due,
I stand in awe of You.

Index of First Lines

Titles which differ from first lines are shown in italics